Got Inspiration?

INSPIRATION DOES THE MIND GOOD

LISA HEAD

PAGE PUBLISHING, INC.
New York, NY

First originally published by Page Publishing, Inc. 2016

ISBN 978-1-68348-409-7 (Paperback)
ISBN 978-1-68348-410-3 (Digital)

Photograph credit: Photography by Thomas Boss

Printed in the United States of America

Accidents Happen

We all hear this saying "accidents happen." We all have had them. They do happen and they are defined as accidents because they are unexpected and unplanned. Many are minor. Think about some accidents you've had. Most are probably minor and have not changed much about your life. I've had many that I would describe this way. From slipping on the ice during my life's worth of Michigan winters to a couple of car accidents as a young driver, many accidents I've had have not changed much, if anything, about my life. This changed one day in 2013.

I had an accident on my bicycle and suffered a traumatic brain injury. How many times, especially as a young child, have you wiped out on your bike? As a child, most accidents may have resulted in a scraped knee. This put me in a coma. Much more serious. I am still working on my recovery. I attend therapy and see a few different doctors. Hopeful, but I still have a "road" ahead of me.

The worst bicycle accident I had witnessed occurred when I was young. My cousin actually was riding a bike of mine that she had taken without permission. I yelled at her for taking it and she turned to stick her tongue out at me. At this moment, she crashed. The impact of her crash was her biting her tongue off! Trauma for sure. My neighbor was a nurse and we got my cousin help right away. It was a bad accident, but did not change much about her life long term. She still had enough of her tongue as a youngster and adult that the accident didn't have much of a long term impact. We shall see about mine.

I believe a couple of dogs barking angrily at each other and an odd spot on the bridge I tried to ride across, contributed to my accident but I don't know. I will never know and really it does not matter. What does matter is my life changed that day. I went from being a teacher, mother, wife, friend, church council member, responsible adult, to being in a coma, to being what and who I am today. A work in progress for sure!

CHAPTER 1

Inspiration Is Integral to Our Lives

Inspiration

Inspiration is about how the mind reacts to a stimulus. We usually think of inspiration in a positive way, which is what most of my writing at this point will be about. Inspiration can result in positive emotions. Quite often it does. It can also lead to positive action. Being inspired leads to many things, including art, entertainment, music, charity, friendship, love, your profession, your choices. These things make us who we are and the way we become. Happiness and positive influences lead us in a positive direction.

I was inspired at young ages by family, friends, and teachers. This, in my case, led to mostly good memories, grades, experiences, and choices. I had loving, hardworking, supportive parents. My older brother was well-liked, handy, full of energy and lust for life. My sister was creative, fashionable, fun, and always had friends.

It would be exhausting and unnecessary to go into poor choices or good of friends or family members. I would like to say both sides of my family exposed me to love and experiences that positively impacted family and individuals. Or people that helped their environment, animals, and/or community. There are those, also, to learn from experience what individual poor choices could do. I saw this first hand as well. Of course, poor choices affect individuals and those that are a part of their life. So do positive choices and experiences of individuals.

My life has not always been easy or filled with good choices on my part. There were (and still are) negative people in my life. I was blessed by enough to begin on a positive path. Despite negatives, I graduated high school with honors and attended Michigan State University. I chose to become an elementary school teacher there. I was hired by a very good school district and have many positive memories from my years of teaching. I was, also, blessed to meet again, date, fall in love, and marry a classmate from junior high school (now middle school). We had two amazing children and many incredible experiences.

My journey continued with an active role at school, in my family, and with my church. I taught Sunday school and became a member of my church's council. The work serving my church started a path I wanted for my children led to a few years of wonderful memories, and to more recipients of my personal inspiration. From my very personable pastor to people that did many deeds to help others and our community. For example, a member of the choir and his amazing choir director/organist wife run a program for those in need in Detroit. Their work feeds and clothes people that are in need. We, as a church community, raise money for children, families, and the local community. We are part of the Crop Walk for Hunger every year. When I was fortunate enough to participate in Susan G. Komen's 3 Day, my church was a big part of my fund-raising. Being a part of a church family can lead to wonderful experiences for many individuals.

Multiple Inspiration

Inspiration changes and should change as you grow and change. Even writing about inspiration is evolving. There are so many people to be challenged or inspired by. Every day you can find people to be inspired by that you knew nothing about the day before. It is a positive that there are so many sources of inspiration. Each person has a host of choices to make in regard to this topic. Of course, your choices have a huge range. They can be from a story making you smile and turn with a positive outlook to your next interaction with someone to becoming involved in something.

Members of our armed forces, hospital and teaching staffs, police and fire departments for example are more than worthy of inspiration, gratitude, and admiration. Veterans that volunteer and work with other veterans are incredible. Usually there is a personal connection, not to diminish positive action in anyway, however service or action is a blessing. Stories can be found everywhere. Your personal inspiration can result in your action. This can mean helping others in some way. The "size" of your support does not matter. Positive action leads to positive results for others and yourself.

I had a close family related reason for participating in Susan G. Komen's 3 Day, but reason or no I still raised that money and did that amazing walk for a very worthwhile reason. If I could I would do it again. I walked with an incredible group of women. We had amazing, fun, funny support from crowds of people as we went. The memories alone made that walk worth it. That involves a very large group of people.

There are many people who use their platforms to help others. Jobs in the public eye can be a way to do this service. The people could be with a local organization or affiliated with local television. Many people help or inspire others. Dr. Oz, for example, helps countless numbers of people. He informs people of many ways to be healthy. His program also celebrates individuals that have found success and can share their own stories. Of course he reaches many, however others do this on a more local level. God bless everyone who is where they are for positive action of any kind.

Amy Purdy is amazing! What she has done for others, her sport, and organization cannot be underestimated. I was in a bad place personally when "the world" became acquainted with her. However, I have read her book. Her story became part of many lives when she danced on Dancing with the Stars. Her partner was Derek Hough. He has won the trophy multiple times. He made it to the finals with Amy Purdy. She has also won medals snowboarding. Her legs are prosthetic legs yet she was able to accomplish these and other fetes. She has an incredible support system and is worthy of their support. Many people are worthy that do not have the people in their lives, hopefully you can become inspired and work to bring yourself and/or others some peace and comfort. This may come about by pursuing your passion while helping others. Read her book. It is well worth reading.

I wish to highlight several individuals in the next sections. Some of these fine individuals I have admired and been inspired by for years. Others I have learned more about and/or grown to be inspired by over my personal recovery journey. If I wrote this book at another time, many (although I'm sure not all) of the people would be different. The point in sharing why they inspire me is not to say they should be your personal inspiration. I am focusing in on these people to share why I feel they are worthy and motivate me to work harder. Look for the good in others and make the conscious choice to be your best self every day. Inspiration can impact your personal journey and experience on our planet.

As mentioned, you can find inspiration all over. Focusing on inspirational people can help you get through tough times in life. From spiritual leaders like Gandhi to musicians such as Trace Adkins or Bono to fitness experts like Peter Nielson, you can find peace and inspiration in the lives of others. The celebrity Nick Cannon was inspired by his own personal history and love of reading to write a children's book. This book continues to pass on the love of reading to his own children, as well as, others. He also spends time at a children's hospital. His support of this hospital and the time he spends at it benefit these children and their families in many ways including sharing his love of children's literature. Focusing on the positive can benefit you in small ways or it can help to change your life and others' lives in big ways.

Books and authors can be a source of inspiration. When I was a child, I loved, learned, and spent family time with books. When I was a bit older, I began reading Stephen King. People generally know him as a master of horror. He is well-known for the horror genre, but has written in many genres. His work includes novels, short stories, screenplays, newspaper columns, and so much more. Several family members, including my wonderful mother, read Stephen King. As I learned more about him as a husband and man I grew to be inspired by him as well.

Inspiration can be found in many places. You may find inspiration in your daily life. People that do amazing things are all over. You may find yours at church, in a religious or social group, at your job, on television, in a magazine or newspaper, or another place. Where it's found is not as important as what you do with it. Positive thoughts and action lead to positive thoughts and action.

During my years teaching, I found many people who inspired me. Many of my co-workers were not only teaching but also inspiring a love of learning. From teachers I teamed with for programs to those that I learned from or worked with daily, teachers can make schools amazing places to be a part of. I realize people do have bad experiences, however I can honestly state that I was truly blessed. Students I've had over the years enriched my experience as well. Funny, smart, athletic, kind, thoughtful, skilled, all kinds of qualities and strengths of children I've had the pleasure to teach. Of course, I have had bad experiences as well, however the good far outweighs the bad!

CHAPTER 2

My Current Inspiration

I want to include the following famous sources of inspiration because they have meant a lot to me. You may know a lot about these individuals already. Here I try to highlight why they have been inspirational to me. Hopefully you can relate to my inspiration and use it to lighten or enrich your life.

Ellen DeGeneres

"Be kind to one another."

This multi-talented woman ends each of her talk show programs with the five words I have included above. She has said this more than many people have said "please" or "thank you." Just as many people need to increase their use of words like please and thank you, we do also need to be kind to one another. Ellen DeGeneres is kind to others. She lives her life supporting causes she believes in, as well as, being kind to others.

Ellen is happily married to Portia de Rossi. She was a pioneer to live her life with the woman that she loves. Her personal strength and love have inspired the strength of many in the LGBT community.

People that are heterosexual have grown in their understanding/comfort with the homosexual and transgender community. Ellen makes the choice to live her best self and being true to herself is one monumental way she accomplishes this task.

Ellen also truly loves animals. She has pets that are much-loved members of her household. She shares many videos with animals as the stars on her television show and on her online program. She is, also, an amazing humanitarian. She contributes both time and money to dozens of organizations. She serves on the board of directors of charitable organizations. Her help and support go beyond a couple of hours and a bit of money. Her work has led to awareness and action in many others.

Hundreds of pages could be written about the positive impact she has made over the last few decades. I am not going to do that, however I do want to mention some examples of her best self as shown on her television program.

Many people have been given things or money on her show. Sometimes it's because they play a fun game on her show. Sometimes it's having a lucky seat or dancing and showing delight. Other times, there are what one could say more profound reasons for her love, support, and generosity. One woman in her early thirties with cancer came on the show with family members. She was helped with money and a new vehicle. I believe this meant more than the financial help. Ellen was being kind. She made sure there was support.

Inspiration, of course, is not limited to adults. Children are celebrated on her show as well. Sometimes Ellen and her show take children places, like a museum, other times children appear as a guest on her show. One young girl was celebrated by Ellen on her show, but this girl showed how Ellen inspired her. This young pianist has played Carnegie Hall multiple times. Amazing fete. She, in turn, wrote a piano piece about Ellen. It was incredible!

Be kind to one another.

Michael Strahan

"Nothing is impossible. The word itself says I'm possible."
—Audrey Hepburn

I felt the above quote a fitting one for Michael Strahan. This is a man who, from "somewhat humble" beginnings, has risen to super-stardom. He has achieved success in more arenas than most people achieved in one. He had a tremendous professional football career. He played for the New York Giants during his fifteen-year career as a defensive end. He received numerous awards. They won a Super Bowl while he was part of the team. He has been inducted into the Football Hall of Fame. He has also achieved success on television and film. Parts of his busy life and work have included being in commercials, films, web series, and hosting award shows. He is currently a talk show cohost. He shares snippets of his life, current events, facts (fun and otherwise), and opinions with his audience. Michael is, also, a father, friend, and co-worker to many.

What many people may not know about him is he was not put on his path at a very young age. While this has been a positive/supportive path for many children, it has also been destructive for many children as well. Children are, at times, forced into a sport and pushed beyond their capabilities. Parenting is tough. Many parents think they are doing the right things in regards to sports but they are not. Just as Kelly Ripa and Michael Strahan debate many parenting issues on their show Live with Kelly and Michael, parenting decisions are often debated and can be incredibly tough. Regardless, Michael was raised in a supportive home. His parents, as well as other family members, were/are athletes. His father was also a member of our military. They were stationed in Germany when Michael was a teenager. Michael lived in Germany, however the decision for Michael to move back to the United States and to move in with his uncle was made.

It was then that Michael began playing football on his high school team. With hard work and support, he went on to a successful and award winning college then professional career.

Michael was blessed with talent, but he also worked very hard. Michael's uncle had experience to share with him. His uncle played defensive end at Texas Southern University. Michael followed in his uncle's footsteps and did the same. He worked with and through injuries. He chose to do this. People in his life helped and supported him. He followed through. He took his talent, support, personal inspiration, and opportunities to a level that made him successful. I do not believe he would minimize the impact other people have made in his life. Every day, every person has the choice to go with what they have or to do other things. His choices have led to where he is and people should realize how important individual choices can be to your life.

Michael continues to inspire others. Many athletes could attest to this fact. It is not only athletes that he has helped or supported. Michael turned his home over to support others. People took tours of his home. The money went to good causes. He raised money for those in need in many instances/ways. Many young people and families have benefitted from his support/involvement in charities. The incredible Barbara Walters named him one of the Ten Most Fascinating of the Year 2014. He continues to "reinvent" himself. He reaches people, multiple groups of people, through his work. Children, aging individuals, young adults, daytime television viewers, multiple groups of people benefit from his work.

Oprah Winfrey

> "My mission in life is not merely to survive, but to thrive. And to do so with some passion, some compassion, some humor, and some style."
> —Maya Angelou

Oprah Winfrey does a lot more today than merely survive. She is, after all, a billionaire. She does not just live a rich life. I believe, despite being able to just live a life of pure indulgence, she still lives with passion, compassion, humor, and style. It is true that she has multiple homes and can buy anything she wishes to buy. However, she still works. She takes on projects, has her own television network and production company. Oprah cares about how people feel. She reaches many through the program "Oprah & Deepak Manifesting True Success." This is meditation for a journey to guide each person to thrive.

Childhood was very different for her than her life today. Life was a trail and struggle. Oprah had a single, poor, young mother. She lived in multiple places with different people as she grew up. She suffered. She had to persevere much during her young life. There were despicable and hurtful people in her life. She was blessed with many talents and abilities, as well as, a caring, loving grandmother. Oprah persevered and worked hard to become what and who she is today.

Her radio then television talk show broke ground. A full-figured African-American woman with a successful program was unthinkable. She not only had success, her television talk show changed the format of television talk shows. The focus of her shows became self-improvement. There was focus on celebrity, spirituality, and literature. Her book clubs not only created successful authors, but also gave people tools for self-improvement. She has shown that she cares about people.

She supported many individuals. Ellen DeGeneres, and many others in the LGBT community, came out on her show. A whole audience full of courageous people came out on one program. Her political support, including that of Barack Obama has had tremendous impact on politics and influence on lives. Her humanitarian efforts are substantial.

People for the Ethical Treatment of Animals (PETA) has been a recipient of her generosity, as so have many young women, in the

United States as well as in Africa. She has given and raised money for multiple causes. Hurricane relief was greatly spurred by her efforts. Oprah has helped in times of disaster and individual need.

Of course her work has not only had impact on our society, it has also added to her celebrity. The Oprah Effect is what some have termed humanity's reaction to Oprah bringing attention to something. Her impact can be felt or traced throughout the world. That something can be charity. It can also be a political cause or self-improvement, be it education or spirituality.

Oprah has received multiple awards. Her work and earnings have put her on many lists. She is a part of all of our lives in some way. She is now a historical figure. From the impoverished girl who wore potato sack dresses to the icon she became. She has survived with passion and compassion (and humor and style).

Jennifer Lopez

"Believe you can and you're halfway there."
—Theodore Roosevelt

Jennifer Lopez believed in herself and turned herself into what and who she is today. She, also, did have support and a seemingly loving family. She lived in a modest apartment with her parents and siblings. Her parents supported her in many things and in many ways. However, as traditional Puerto Rican parents, they initially did not believe a young Hispanic girl should pursue show business.

I do not know who Jennifer Lopez was inspired by as a child or young adult. It is clear that she is worthy of inspiration. She believed in herself and followed the path she wanted to follow. She danced and sang and acted. She continues to dance and sing and act. She has struggled at times personally and professionally. People have discouraged her at times. She continues to follow/blaze her own path.

Sites about her list her occupation as actress, author, dancer, fashion designer, producer, singer, and songwriter. Wow! Not only can you wear clothing and perfume from one of her lines, you can listen to her music or watch a video that she is in. From dancing on one television program to being a celebrity judge on another or acting in many films, Jennifer Lopez, or as she's commonly known JLo, is a superstar. She has earned her place on many top lists, including being named most influential Hispanic People en Español.

Of course, there are many reasons to admire or be inspired by Jennifer Lopez. Her talents and hard work are commendable. Jennifer works hard. From her voice to her dancing, acting, and candor/support of other talented individuals to achieve their dreams, JLo has made a difference. She chose to give back as well. With her sister, she explored charities with which to become involved. Family influenced her involvement. Not only was a sister of hers a partner in this venture, but she was also influenced by her ex-sister-in-law's fight for life.

This and a scary experience with her own daughter led to what eventually has become Lopez Family Foundation. Jennifer realized parents needed more resources. While enduring a health scare with her own daughter, she did not need to worry about money at all. Other parents do have money to worry about or stop them from getting the help they need. Jennifer Lopez wanted to help to relieve monetary pressures for parents when getting medical help for their children. The foundation helps mothers by providing more quality health care as well as health education. This work has led entire communities to raising healthy children. Her personal struggles led to positive action for many families.

Keanu Reeves

"The truth is you don't know what is going to happen tomorrow.
Life is a crazy ride, and nothing is guaranteed."
—Eminem

Keanu Reeves is an accomplished actor. He has entertained millions of people. Depending on the movie, you may be laughing or sitting anxiously on the edge of your seat. I have done both. His life has been tough or even tragic at times. At a young age, his father left his family and Keanu eventually lost contact with him entirely. Keanu also struggled in school. He has dyslexia and, although he reads a lot now, learning to read was a struggle.

As an adult, Keanu lost other members of his inner circle. River Phoenix, who was a very dear friend, died of a drug overdose. Keanu struggled through this loss. He did fall in love. The love of his life at this time became pregnant. Keanu Reeves was going to be a father. Unfortunately at eight months, his child was stillborn. Less than two years later, his love and the mother of his lost child died in a car accident.

I am sure these events affected who he was and who he is today. Life is and can be a crazy ride. However, Keanu Reeves is a good man. He is a humanitarian. He is a charitable actor. He gives to those around him. He has split his paychecks from blockbuster movies with other actors as well as members of the set.

Philanthropy, or humanitarianism, is caring, nourishing, developing, and enhancing life. The benefits of being a philanthropist or humanitarian go both ways. People on his movie sets and other recipients have benefitted, however I am sure that Keanu Reeves has as well. We each can help others and enrich our own lives at the same time.

Drew Barrymore

"Whoever is happy will make others happy too."
—Anne Frank

Drew Barrymore makes other people happy. Many of her movies are romantic comedies. These, along with the other movies she has starred in, entertain and make other people happy. She has appeared in both movies and on television. She, also, has appeared as a spokesperson. She is known as an actress, author, producer, director, and model. Her work results in smiles, laughs, and many other positive emotions/reactions.

Part of the reason I have included her here in these pages is because of her positive impact in my own life. Over the years, I am close to her age; I have seen her on television, in the movies, in magazines, many outlets. She comes across as a very positive person. While recovering, I saw a favorite movie of mine that she starred in. I had a traumatic brain injury. I have seen and enjoyed the movie 50 First Dates many times. Her character suffered a brain injury. During the movie, the characters meet other brain injury victims. Seeing this movie while recuperating in a nursing home just about the time of my fortieth birthday was a different experience. I related to all of these injured patients in a new way. It still made me happy though.

Drew has chosen a very worthy cause to support with time and money. Her ties and support go to the UN World Food Program (WFP). They have named her an ambassador against hunger. Her involvement inspires others to donate time and money. The charity was built to provide food through a branch of the United Nations. The WFP provides food to ninety million people per year. Of that number, fifty-eight million are children.

In her books about her own life, people can have a glimpse into what growing up as part of a famous family is like. Life, as people say, isn't easy. The money and fame was abundant, but so were people that exposed Drew as a young child to indulgence and self-centeredness. Everyone goes through trials and triumphs. Positive people and happiness can truly spread a positive outlook and happiness to others however. Try to focus on happiness. I know I need to at this time especially.

Barack Obama

"No matter what people tell you, words
and ideas can change the world."
—Robin Williams

Many inspirational things have been said and written about Barack Obama. He is, after all, the forty-fourth President of the United States of America. I've read much literature and recommend everyone reading about his life and presidency. I felt this quote from the great Robin Williams was incredibly fitting. Barack Obama has changed the world. Whether you agree politically with this president or you do not, his election and years in office have changed the world.

The Audacity of Hope: Thoughts on Reclaiming the American Dream is one of the books written by Barack Obama. This book's origin can be traced back. A former pastor of the president was moved by and inspired by a painting. This painting inspired a sermon that President Obama was moved and inspired by. His thoughts and reflection on the sermon led to an impactful keynote address that Mr. Obama gave as a then senator at a Democratic National Convention. This speech catapulted Barack Obama's career and fame. The audacity of hope highlights people from different periods of time and in different situations. What these people share is an uncertain future. In America, they also share an audacity of hope. Inspiration can be found.

His background and life in many different areas affected who he is today. The people he has known, as diverse as they are, affected who he is today. Every choice he has made, ideas he has shared, movements/work he has been involved in affected who he is today. In turn, his life and presidency have affected society and each of our individual lives.

This is and throughout history has been a world divided. Tracing back through history, division can be found. At times it has been division between races. Other times it has been another difference that has separated or pitted people against each other. We do work through issues. Oftentimes, other issues arise. Unfortunately it appears to be human nature. Inspirational people like Barack Obama prove that we do have the ability to improve or work beyond divisions.

Mr. Barack Obama lived the early years of his life with his Kenyan father and white mother. He was born in Hawaii. Living in Hawaii during his childhood exposed him to different cultures and a different perspective than he would have been exposed to in the continental United States. His mother and father divorced leading to remarriages and half-brothers and sisters for Barack. Barack went on to academic success and accolades. His work at prestigious universities led to work in Chicago. This led to Michelle (who became his wife and the mother of their girls) and to his work in government.

His work as a politician and author has led to monetary riches as well. He gives back. One of the charities he donates a considerable amount to, Fisher House Foundation, is for veterans and their families. His success from early days of registering African-American voters to changing programs and laws on a national level is obviously impressive. He has changed the world.

His words and ideas, thoughts and actions have changed the United States of America and the rest of the world.

CHAPTER 3

Both Positive and Negative

The Power of the Mind

The mind is truly powerful. Your mind shapes your life. Your mind has the power to change your life. Setting goals and identifying steps on the way to reaching your goals is powerful. People can do many things they set out to do. People can, also, "fall into" their roles in life. Sometimes a seemingly small step or decision is made and one finds himself/herself on a path. Whether this "turns out" to be positive or negative, you still have the power or choice to continue on your path or to change direction.

We all have our minds. Some people are smarter than others. Some people are more attractive than others. Some people are more athletic, or better singers, or dancers, or are more charismatic. Whatever your strengths or weaknesses, each person has their mind. The choices someone is capable of making may not be on the same level as another person's choices, however choices are still made.

As everyone seems to be aware of the fact that poor choices can be made, not everyone gives much credence to influences in our choices. People do have and "dole out" a lot of excuses. People blame many things for their choices from something another person does to the weather. No one seems to have a lack of excuses. However, people often go for the easy answer. To examine, explain, and work with the consequences of choices is, often, more difficult. Most of the time, people can do without the excuses. Everyone does not need to know why every choice a person makes is their choice. At times in history and in everyone's daily life, people are influenced by someone else. Sometimes you can be "taken advantage of" by someone with a smooth pitch. People that work in sales, for example, do pitch products for a living. These people may also believe in the product they are working to sell. Either way, influences do affect people's choices.

Charles Manson

"Helter Skelter"

Charles Manson has certainly influenced people's choices. Unfortunately, he still does. This man had a family of followers that committed horrific acts including multiple murders. He promoted his manifesto. His delivery, lifestyle, sex, and drugs led to and aided in his actions and the actions of other people in his family. Family is what he chose to call their group because of the power of that word alone. Many people in his family were runaways. They were people that were alone before joining his family.

"Helter Skelter" from The Beatles' White Album was used by Charles Manson. This man was a charismatic orator. He used the music of The Beatles and even passages from the Bible to promote his cause. He convinced others of a forthcoming apocalyptic race riot. He compared the young long-haired musicians in the Beatles to Jesus Christ. He used the lyrics to manipulatively inspire members of the family. Family members would hear this music repeatedly for hours. They would also write, play music, do drugs, and listen to Charles Manson.

Charles Manson did not have love, support, and family growing up. Neither do many other people that do not make the choices that he made. His early years were spent living with his young mother or his aunt and uncle. While with his mother, they went from one shoddy hotel to the next. She was an alcoholic. They both committed petty crimes for money. His mother even sold him once for beer. His aunt and uncle got him back. It seems that being a teenager led to more crime, which resulted in him being incarcerated in a series of institutions.

He broke out of or ran away from multiple institutions. He used and manipulated music, lyrics, groups making news, stories, and even religion to influence himself and others to be a part of his family. The power of the mind is incredible. He may not have scored his exact intelligence on the IQ test he took, however his score of a hundred and nine is close to the one hundred score, which is average. If he had the impact he had on society, everyone should realize the power of the mind. Promote, influence, inspire change in a positive direction.

Adolf Hitler

"Heil Hitler" & *"Mein Kampf"*

Here is another example of a single person who rose to power and controlled thoughts and actions of many. The greeting of *Heil* became a mantra. Shouts of *Heil* Hitler showed support. Waving of his swastika flag showed support. His writings in *Mein Kampf* were used to inspire many things. What he saw as his struggle led to the deaths of millions of people, many of them for no other reason than because they were Jewish.

Adolf Hitler's father had a path in mind for his son. Adolf did not agree with his father. He wanted different things for himself. Adolf did poorly, he claims purposely poor, at his school because he wanted to go to another school. Many childhood and issues during his early years were due to this conflict with his father. His father had a practical path laid out and Adolf wanted to follow his art. This led to living on his own doing odd jobs as a young adult. His next step was military service. Adolf served Germany during World War I. He gained attention and military accolades during this war.

Adolf promoted anti-Semitism and anti-communism with Nazi propaganda. He was charismatic and gained a following. More and more as time went on. He became a powerful and influential leader. He wanted to eliminate Jewish people from Germany and change the results of what he saw as the injustices that resulted from World War I. This led to World War II and the Holocaust. Millions of people died. Millions of Jewish people and others seen as racially inferior were murdered because they were Jewish or deemed inferior. Millions of people that had nothing to do with politics or war died. Millions died because they were Jewish. Millions of people died fighting World War II. Adolf Hitler and the woman he loved, Eva Braun, committed suicide.

Many things could and have been said about Hitler. The acts committed were beyond deplorable. His early years influenced who he was and what he became, however he is responsible. Others have had similar trials and suffered on their path, yet still made it through life without causing so much devastation. He wasn't alone, he had many who swore allegiance to him and what they tried to accomplish. However, he chose his path and believed in what he was doing. The so-called mob mentality led many people to commit horrendous acts. Every person needs to think beyond what they are "caught up" in. At times, loved ones need to help others.

Currently there are terrorist groups who have what seems to be mob mentality. Groups of people are doing horrendous acts to further their cause. People are on both sides. There are those who are caught up and inspired to be part and those who are on the other side. People are defending themselves from terror, protecting themselves and others, or cautiously observing events.

CHAPTER 4

My Accident and Inspiration

My story

I have always tried to live my life with balance. I wanted to follow thru with commitments and responsibilities. I wanted to follow what I believed was a moral path. Fun, love, and passion played a huge part of my life as well. Being a good parent, wife, mother, teacher, relative, and friend all had a part in this balance.

My intentions were/are always good I believe. However, I suffered an accident. Yes, it was an accident, but that doesn't stop me from going through every action I took that day. Realistically I know there are actions that I took and a few actions I didn't take that may have led to or prevented my accident. What's done is done however. As much as I struggle or as tough as things are for others, this is what life is right now. Now my job is to get back what I can. To do and be what I can.

One busy day in June of 2013, I took my bicycle for a ride. It had been a day booked with activities. My husband and children were at home. They were doing other things. I have heard different accounts of the time before my ride and I don't remember. What I do know is that I rode my bicycle over to my brother's house. He lives a couple of neighborhoods away. A short ride really. My brother was not at home. It was a busy day for him as well. On my return trip was when I crashed my bike.

Leaving my brother's neighborhood, there is a paved path that leads to a bridge which goes over a river. The path that leads to the bridge goes down a hill through a small patch of woods. This much I know … I wrecked on this bridge. I suffered a traumatic brain injury. I think I was distracted by music and barking dogs from the house on the river, but I don't know if this is a true memory. It doesn't matter really. My accident was witnessed by a man canoeing down the river. I have never seen anyone canoe this river, yet he was and he called 911 on my behalf. While being treated by the fire fighter from emergency dispatch, my husband and he spoke on my cell phone. Of course I don't remember this either. My husband knew the man from school being a fire fighter himself.

I was transported to the hospital and was in a coma for over a week. My husband, children, parents, friends, and other relatives were in the visitor role at the hospital. I had some wonderful care including a nurse who did my hair, to my mother reading to me. I was in the hospital on my son's birthday, but managed a thumbs-up for him. Recovery was and continues to be a step by step process. I went from a coma to just being awake to being able to do little things again. I went from one hospital to another to Detroit Medical Center to a nursing home with rehabilitation before going home. This led to outpatient rehab. I am still on my journey.

My eyes are an issue, I am told, that only time will resolve. Nerves were severed by my accident, so my eyes do not work the way they should. People seem to understand my description of my sight as tunnel vision. All I know is surgery is not an option and nerves grow back extremely slowly. My eyes throw off other rehabilitation as well. Since I cannot see like I once could, I find other things difficult that I don't believe I would have. As I write, I'm in a wheelchair. I use a walker for short distances like going to the bathroom. I have used my walker in and out of a few places. My first walks were the book club I was in at my aunt and uncle's church and my own church on Easter morning of 2014. My left side is not really useful. I can move my limbs, but I don't have the control or use of them that I used to have. I'm a lifelong left-handed person having to write with her right hand. I am typing with my right hand only as well.

I have heard many inspiring stories since my accident. One woman, for example, recovered from a traumatic brain injury to go on to medical school. She defied the odds and is still doing very well. Not everyone is encouraging or wants to share an inspiring story. One doctor, who told my father I was going to die in the hospital, told me recently that I would not recover further. He was quoting text on recovery from traumatic brain injury and told me twelve to fourteen months was the recovery window. I do not plan on seeing him again. I'm too young for this to be it.

As a teacher (I am even though I cannot currently teach), I understand saying things carefully due to the possibilities of legal consequences or simply giving an inaccurate portrayal of a situation. However this doctor did not have to say this like he did. He could have said I may not get some abilities back or even that I may always have my wheelchair to use when needed. There was no reason to say my recovery window was closed. I was not even asking him to make recovery predictions. A stubborn part of me wants to prove him wrong and giving him huge benefit maybe he knew it would. I believe he meant what he said though. He needs to think like a patient to be a better doctor. Think of others before you open your mouth, are words to live by. I prefer to follow inspiration and people who illicit inspiration.

My Aunt Rose is an example of someone who has used humor and perseverance to become someone another person can be inspired by. Now well over a decade ago, my hilarious and loving aunt found out she had brain cancer. She had to have a tumor that had grown removed. This, of course, changed many things in her life. She is my mother's sister. As much of my mother's family does, she lives about four hours away from us. She lives close too much of my mother's family. She has a wonderful, hardworking, funny husband. She has two children and many friends. Going to Rose's was always a promise of a good, comfortable time. Rose has suffered many seizures since her surgery. Yet she still does most everything she wants to do and works around her obstacles. While she is an inspiration, she does not always take the best care of herself. She takes care of others, including my grandmother during the last years of her life. She does not make the best choices for herself though. She is a smoker and a diet cola drinker. Besides these two vices, she does not eat like she should or follow all of her doctors' advice/orders. She clearly loves others and is a wonderful aunt (mother, grandmother, sister, wife, and friend).

Most everyone can find someone in their family who can inspire them. The range is great, from someone who is smart with money or a good cook to someone who stays true to a strong belief. Again, the impact this makes in your life can vary. You make the choice to lead your life in the way that you do. Of course, when you are a child in the eyes of the law, you have other people that impact your choices. Adults still have laws, bosses, and obligations that impact their choices. People that come into or go out of your life have impact as well. Even advertising or fads impact your life. If you focus on positive inspiration even in difficult times you can stay on a good path.

My life is difficult. I know it could be worse. I have many negative thoughts and at times wish for negative things for myself. Honestly most of the time when negative things enter my mind, they are essentially easier than life as I now know it. I still believe in following the moral path that I laid out for myself. Being a mother has a major influence on my actions as it always has had. At times, people need to question choices before them and be sure they make choices for what they believe, truly believe, is the right path for them. Remember, you do not want to "find" yourself on a path that is not right for you. Look to/follow inspiration.

I do not believe someone like Charles Manson or Adolf Hitler found themselves on a path, however some of the people that were part of their lives may have. This does not excuse them from committing horrendous acts. Even where there is pressure, adults have choices. The glorified or dictated ends do not justify the means. Everyone must, at times, forge their own path. Some of the positive inspirational individuals outlined here did just that. They became what they did by making decisions that helped them achieve what they have in life.

Influences and inspiration grow and change just as you do throughout your life. Even as an adult, you do and should grow and change. Most of us have seen a movie where the main character runs into someone who hasn't changed. This can be fun for a second for the main character, but soon becomes funny or pathetic. Life and things that happen affect who you become. This does not change the fact that you have choices. One way or another change happens. Be true to yourself.

Before my accident, as a teacher, I had the choice to bring my children to my school or to have them go to their home school. I brought them to my school. This was the best choice. I still believe it was the best choice. Due to this choice and my accident, my children had to change schools this year. I had the pleasure to have my daughter for second and third grade. She went on to fourth grade in a dear friend's class. My son was then in my second grade class. The plan was the same, and I was set to teach him and most of his classmates third grade. My accident changed that, however we chose for them to continue in the district where I taught last year. It worked out. Two wonderful friends who work for the district helped. This year, however, it was time for them to attend their home schools. Of course there is good and bad with this choice, but it really makes a lot more sense. Since my daughter is now in middle school, it meant different schools for them anyway.

While going to their school last year to pick them up, I heard an interesting exercise on the radio. The question put out to the listening audience was if you could invite four people to dinner who would they be. The people could be living or dead. Celebrities and politicians made the "guest lists." Many people calling in wished for a dearly departed member of their family. Others wished for inspiring or life changing historical figures. I found this both entertaining and thought provoking. I began to wonder who my loved ones would invite. This included singers, actors, athletes, and departed family members. Whoever would be on your guest list could be very different. As different as they are, you pick them for a reason that means a lot to you. Be it entertainment or intellectual curiosity, you are making a choice to spend time with them. They could be where to look for inspiration.

Inspiration can come from anywhere. Live life with the best in mind. There is a much loved (and joked around with) custodian at the elementary school I worked at. He does his job, is always there, and is a well-liked and respected by staff. Kids love him. One day in the cafeteria, he went from Mr. Russ to a lifesaver. A student I taught and loved was eating his lunch. All of a sudden, he started to choke. Panic and fright ensued. The commotion, thankfully, caught Mr. Russ' attention. Mr. Russ responded. He gave my former student the Heimlich maneuver. It was a success! The student coughed up the food that was choking him. Mr. Russ did get credit for his heroics. The media and members of the community spread the story. Mr. Russ is a hero. My previous mention of teaching staff includes everyone who works at a school. Just as everyone who works with a police or fire department deserve credit. There are those worthy of respect and admiration everywhere.

Another story that gained worthwhile attention during my recovery was about a man who walked to work without fail daily for years. He walked because he had to walk in order to get to work. He didn't have a car. Although part of his route included bus service and he occasionally got a ride, buses or rides could not take him from his door to his place of work every work day. As a full-time employee, he spent many hours walking. He walked many miles in all kinds of weather. This man is worthy of the attention his story gained and the car he ended up getting.

Looking for inspiration does not mean looking at the world with "rose colored glasses." This common phrase is more than trying to see the best in everything or everyone. If you look at everything through "rose colored glasses" you can miss important facts. People can take advantage of you. People are hurtful at times. People can hurt you. They may be hurting someone to better themselves in some way, but it doesn't matter. It doesn't make it okay. Be realistic. Someone can find themselves in a bad situation by being too trusting. However, someone can find themselves in a bad situation by being too distrustful. Balance. At times there is a fine line. The best you can do at times is to be realistic and hope for the best.

Currently I am still working hard to be more self-sufficient. My friends who haven't seen me recently always remark on my improvements. My best friend from high school remarked on my physical improvements since she had last seen me during our most recent visit. During my last telephone conversation with one of my dearest co-workers and friends, it was how good our conversation was that she found to "be like old times." I know changes are harder for me to recognize so it is wonderful to get these reactions. I know I still have a way to go, but it does encourage me that people see changes.

Focusing on how far I've come helps me to believe improvements can still be made.

I have taught Sunday school and Vacation Bible School. I still want to get back to my own classroom, but am glad for these experiences. I enjoy them and believe they've gone well. These experiences definitely keep me focusing on being positive and inspired to live my life in the best way that I possibly can.

Inspiration can be from anywhere. Live your life with the best in mind.

My Story, Conclusion of Sorts

> "It is during our darkest moments that
> we must focus to see the light."
> —Aristotle Onassis

I've been through some dark times in my life. Since I am recovering from a devastating accident, I'm not far from a dark moment in my life today. However, I prefer to think of myself as being in an early hour of the morning. If you have ever camped, you will understand the time of day I am referring to now.

The sun has broken on the horizon. It is quiet. Most of the world is still. Pictures could be taken of nature's beauty outside the tent's flap and you know some people are moving around where you are even though you are momentarily somewhat cozy inside the tent and in your sleeping bag. The rest of the world is moving and doing what needs to be done where they are at the moment. Life goes on and soon those with you on your trip will be moving on as well. If you are in a moment like this you need to focus on the light. The opportunity to enjoy the beauty of nature, to make memories with your companions, and to satisfy your personal needs (and wants) are all right there for you.

Time to focus on the light. Live with the best in mind.

CHAPTER 5

Reaching Others

Social Media

Social media is using the internet on handheld devices, such as cellphones and computers to interact with others. There is a large range of interactions people can participate in. People can simply read the posts of others on a social networking site or they can watch a video on YouTube. Of course people post a variety of their own or others' videos, pictures, and thoughts. When using a social network such as Facebook, your friends on the network react to things that are posted. This allows you to view those postings you may not otherwise see. This way, you see the posts of your friends' friends. If the original post your friend commented on was something you posted, it opens you up to reactions.

People tend to follow human social interaction manners, however they can react as they wish or not at all. People can take people off of their friend lists. This may happen due to an exchange about a post, but does happen for other reasons as well. Posts are put on for a multitude of reasons. Posts can mean a lot to individuals. Going on a social media site can lead to your amusement, entertainment, stress relief, networking, inspiration, etc.

Facebook is currently a big part of my life. It is a welcome distraction and, can be, a source of inspiration. I spend the majority of most days sitting alone in my wheelchair with the television on and my cellphone close by. On Facebook, I read the posts of others and occasionally post something of my own. Not to diminish the importance of any of my friends (friends are essential), but I have to elaborate on two types of posts I look for with relish. By relish I refer to interest and excitement. The prospect of learning, laughing, comfort, and inspiration has me picking up my cellphone.

Posts by my Aunt Donna and Uncle Larry, with whom I have been in the previous mentioned book clubs, post regularly. Sometimes they share family events or something funny. Before retiring, my Uncle Larry worked for Leader Dogs for the Blind and he will repost pictures and articles related to their organization. Often my aunt and uncle put up religious posts. While some people may not appreciate these posts, I do. I find comfort, peace, hope, understanding, and/or inspiration in them.

The other uplifting posts I look for are by a group. My roommate and best friend from college helped me to become a member of this group. My dear friend came over to visit me one day that she wasn't working. She went into the educational field as well. She is now an elementary school principal. We are like-minded on many topics, have a history, and I respect her opinion. While she was visiting I shared my writing and ideas with her. She thought I would appreciate and enjoy being part of the group. She was right! Inspiration is what this group is all about. There are positive articles, exercises to complete, and links to explore if interested.

Social media, like many things, has a good and bad side. People can spend their lives with social media. They can even create avatars and spend all their time in virtual realities. Too much of a good thing is too much. If you are using social media to stay in touch with people, learn something, network for your business or education, or another reason that aligns with your morals, it is part of your life. People can spend too much time however. Social media can be a positive part of your life or it can lead to a negative all-encompassing life.

Make sure to think about what you do. Be sure your actions align with your beliefs. Do not find yourself on a path that is not right for you. Chances are inspiration can help here as well. If you are inspired by something or someone and what you are doing is not getting you closer to it or him/her, then you need to make some changes. Most of the people I am inspired by I will never meet, but that does not change the fact that they enrich my life.

Live with the best in mind.

Another Look

"People respond when you tell them there is a future
in front of you. You can leave your past behind."
—Joel Osteen

"A rebirth of spiritual adversity causes us to become new creatures."
—James E. Faust

"Easter is very important to me, it's a second chance."
—Reba McEntire

I could not settle on a single quote to accompany this part of my writing. All of the quotes I've used are from the site entitled Brainy Quotes. There are many categories of quotes on this site. Reading them is nice, heartwarming, etc. Easter Sunday, I was inspired by the sermon. To me, the sermon was about giving everyone/everything a second chance or a second look.

A founding member/creator of Habitat for Humanity was a man by the name of Millard Fuller. This man accomplished a lot and was honored for it many times during his life. His work gave second chances to many. Homes are built for people who are in need and deserving because of Habitat for Humanity. For a banquet in his honor, it was decided one year that a deserving woman who received a home would give a speech for Mr. Fuller. This woman was nervous but so thankful that she told her tale during this speech.

She was raised in tenement housing, had a child of her own, and still lived a difficult life in tenement housing. When her child went to school in that area, she was given a very poor/dire prediction of his success. Being able to move to a new area, get provided with a home, and begin anew in ways meant a whole new world for herself and her son. Her child struggled to read before, but went on to academic success including straight A grades. Her speech received a standing ovation. Her ovation, and second chance, was well-deserved.

To me, this sermon was not only about how we are all given a second chance. Each of us are given or has chances in life. We can and should look at things with an open mind. Inspiration can and should lead to many things in life. If your focus is on something that does not align with your morals or something that is negative for you, it is time to look again or focus on the positive.

Perseverance

"Great works are performed not by strength but by perseverance."
—Samuel Johnson

"I think you make the best with what you've got, you
know? Sometimes you have very little. And you just try to
rise to higher ground, because you're going to suffer one
way or the other. So you just hope you have the strength
and perseverance and good friends and faith, some kind
of faith, to endure and move on to greener pastures."
—Pierce Brosnan

Perseverance is crucially important in everyone's lives. Of course, we all go through a variety of things or stages in life. Comparing tough times is a lose-lose situation. One person's pain or tough time can be thought of as nothing by someone else. Comparatively, one person cannot imagine surviving something another person did. Keeping perseverance is where strength comes in. The same thing can be said for blessings or positive aspects of life.

As far as the great works mentioned above go, I suppose that is all relative as well. Things I have accomplished in my life mean a lot to me. Another person may or may not think very much of what I hold dear or am proud of.

Right now, my work is getting past this stage of my life. That is where inspiration comes in. I need inspiration. Be it photography, literature, music, my children, friends, family, television, whatever the source, inspiration helps me get through the day. Most of the time, inspiration is much more than a lifeline. Yes, I feel like I need a lifeline at times. That is not meant to be overly dramatic. Tough times have to be gotten through just like everything else. Inspiration creates and sustains.

Commitment is part of perseverance. It can also result from inspiration. At times, people become committed to a charity or cause because of a tragedy in their life. Other times, inspiration is the root. People do break commitments, but if desire is present perseverance can be the key.

Inspiration, perseverance, and commitment are all crucially important to me at this time. Inspiration keeps me going. Perseverance and commitment keep me working. I have exercises that I do and I try to do what I can around the house. I miss teaching. I miss many things, including walking and writing with my left hand. I have to and can continue to work. Trying to stay positive and to keep improving are musts.

Whatever your life brings you, you can stick to a path that is right for you. Everyone has the power and ability to persevere. Stay committed to your personal moral path. Inspiration can support you every step of the way on your path.

CHAPTER 6

Possibilities

Success

> "Success is not final, failure is not fatal: it is
> the courage to continue that counts."
> —Winston Churchill

Roadblocks or bumps in the road during life's journey happen. It is up to each person to ensure that they successfully reach their destination. What you see as a roadblock or bump is yours to traverse. At times during life's journey I have avoided bumps or gone around obstacles. Other times, I've cautiously continued on my path and made it to my destination. Keeping with the metaphor, my accident can be seen as a roadblock. My life as I knew it stopped. I cannot continue on my path the way that I was traveling. I cannot turn around and go back either. My route and destination might be forever changed, yet I have to move on.

Everyone must do this. As everyone says, "Life goes on." Roadblocks or bumps in your road must be dealt with. Your attitude and your experiences are yours. Whether a scenic route or a direct one is taken, our journeys will come to an end eventually. No one knows exactly how much time our journeys will take, so making the best of everything and being positive is our best choice.

As stated above, the courage to continue on our individual paths is what counts. Just like athletes have to finish their games, races, or matches, we all need the courage to continue. Everyone knows a story of a team or player that was counted as out that came back to win. This can be the case with people as well.

Some people have experienced more hardships than others in life. Some of the inspirational individuals I wrote about previously have experienced hardship and trials during their life. They persevered. I, for one, am very grateful for their perseverance.

Conclusion

As previously stated, there are many sources of inspiration and inspiration can grow, change, or come to you any given day. Many celebrities are worthy of inspiration. I've been aware of Miley Cyrus and her career for many years. I've enjoyed the music of her father, Billy Ray Cyrus, for years. I've watched the television show that she starred in many times with my own daughter when she was younger. What I have learned recently is how inspiring Miley Cyrus is as a person. She grew up, apparently, in a loving home with two supportive parents and siblings. Her mother even managed her career. Miley has used her gifts and celebrity status to become an incredible humanitarian. She gives money and spends her time on dozens of charities.

Miley Cyrus has even started her own charity. This charity helps/rescues homeless teens and young people. I recently saw a talk show on which she appeared and she said, "I love myself." She loves herself and helps others to love themselves. That alone is a monumental thing! Love yourself.

At times in life, most people go through a time when loving themselves is very difficult. Try to always remember that it is normal and things do change. Right now, my life is extremely difficult. I cannot change what has happened to me. All I can do is spend each day trying to be the best that I am capable of being. I try to do everything I can to be the best mother, family, and community member. I do my exercises and try to improve my physical issues. I read and play games to try to improve my mental issues and memory. Each day I need to remember to love myself. Remember always to love yourself.

Your inspiration may be a part of your profession. Your inspiration may be a part of your family or social circle. Your inspiration may come from nature. Your inspiration may be from one of your passions, loves, interests, or skills. Wherever your inspiration comes from it is yours to enjoy, build upon, work with, honor.

Perseverance, commitment, your personal morals, and goals, in addition to inspiration are all integral to life. Many things that occur are out of our hands. They will happen regardless of our actions. However, we do have impact. Whether we make something that lasts beyond our lifetime or we are a law abiding citizen that interacts with others in our families or in our jobs, we do have our lives to live. Make the most of your life and do everything you can to be positive and happy.

My Journey Continues

It has been a while since I last wrote. I am still working and striving to full recovery. I walk with a cane at times, but still use my wheelchair daily. I am getting stronger. My optic nerve was severed in the accident, so I need someone with me when I leave the house. I haven't driven since the accident and am unsure of when I will be able to. One of the doctors I've visited explained to me that the nerve will grow back a millimeter a year. My left side is extremely weak. I am left-handed, but now write with my right hand. I do therapy exercises to improve the function of my left side, including my eye. Improvements have happened and I am hopeful for more.

Every day I focus on positive actions. I try to do everything I can for my family. I cook and do other household chores. Even with cooking, there are things I cannot do. I use my crockpot and rice cooker more than the stove. I help with the shopping when I can. My involvement in household chores is very different than before my accident.

My daily routine is filled with reading, writing, exercises, and television for the most part. I write a blog about inspiration every day. I spend hours reading research and writing. I, also, read novels and other books that I enjoy. I do my therapy exercises, squats, lunges, and any other exercises I can manage. I watch television programs that amuse or interest me or sporting events. Family and occasionally other people help fill my days as well.

A crucial fact for me, and I imagine others, is that inspiration is good for my mind. By focusing on something positive every day, I stay more positive than I could ever without it. A daily dose of inspiration helps me and hopefully others that read it.

CPSIA information can be obtained
at www.ICGtesting.com
Printed in the USA
FSOW04n0803240217
31063FS